CHORUS OF THE
UNDERGROUND SEA

PRAISE FOR
CHORUS OF THE UNDERGROUND SEA

Montag's ability to hold the specific gravities of history alongside the ephemeral, the banal, and show how they rub against each other, inform and infect each other, is stunning. There are deep ideas at play in this book, unflinching sojourns through the shadowy interior life, and through the attachments that define us—to a lover, parent, child, to the relentless earth and to our terrifically brief appearance in its epoch. But the ideas are electrified by Montag's wildly generous and surprising use of language, clearly the treasure of a mind that misses little, where "…images stack like busted cars up / to the clouds." And yet, the moments that unfold in these poems are so visceral, so aromatic, they might be playing out in your own backyard. It's a scaffold of courage and intimacy and wildness, this book, with so many moments that feel like a "new animal's holy howl / in a forest with no name."

—**Rebecca Rotert, author of** *Understory*

In lush verse and precise imagery, the many voices that make up *Chorus of the Underground Sea* reveal and reflect the gravity of what it means to be a woman, a lover, a wife, a mother, a sister, a daughter, a witch, an outcast, an artist, a muse. Kassandra Montag brilliantly embodies a multitude of voices that span the centuries, and these poems are equal parts meditation, lamentation, and celebration in their unflinching look at how, for many women, our deepest desires are almost always at odds with the lives we've chosen or been given. Questioning the very nature of desire and choice, Montag's speaker in "Flood Line" muses on her desire for the touch of another man, infusing a wind chime on the porch with her loneliness as "It collides against itself, it jostles / its own corners. It reaches / and reaches for something else," with the speaker lamenting, "When I was young I wanted / to be changed by choice, / not by circumstance. And now / I wonder if they are the same thing." What's so compelling about this collection is that each poem, even as it's grieving what's been lost or unrealized, acknowledges the beauty and the necessity of the people, places, and objects that tether us to our hearts and to this earth. One need only look to the title poem to feel this tension, as Montag writes, "Beneath my feet my ancestors stir, / their fins move soundlessly in water that haunts / all I wanted and never had, for I have disappointed / the depths, have fallen short of its measures. / Still,"—the speaker insists—"that water irrigates my crops / and makes my children grow tall."

—**Sarah McKinstry-Brown, author of** *This Bright Darkness*

Across time and place the many voices collected in these vividly imagined and empathetic lyrics sing to us of loneliness and loss, love and survival. In ekphrastic and persona poems, whether in received or open forms, Montag recreates for us the best kind of history—intimate and unsentimental. In one of my favorites, "Interrupted Supper," she writes of a van Es painting, "…this still life radiates movement, / a haunting of objects by those who left them." Just so, the eloquent poems comprising this fine first collection.

—**Susan Aizenberg, author of** *Quiet City*

Chorus
of the
Underground
Sea

POEMS BY

KASSANDRA MONTAG

WSC PRESS - *Wayne, NE*

ISBN 978-1-7379241-1-1
Published by WSC Press

Edited by Stephanie Marcellus
Cover and layout design by Chad Christensen, Elijah Herrington

Cover art: *Stormy Ship* by Katie Meuser
Author photo: Nancy Kohler

WSC Press
1111 Main Street
Wayne, NE 68787

wscpress@wsc.edu
WSCPRESS.COM

for Don

TABLE OF CONTENTS

IV.

V.

VI.

CHORUS OF THE UNDERGROUND SEA

I.

I Prefer Broken Things

The chipped coffee mug,
sweaters not yet mended,
the farmhouse with no doors or windows,
forever open to time drifting through.
The scar above my son's eyebrow,
mark of a near blinding.

Even your heart,
I prefer it all banged up
and slightly askew—
that raw moment when we cannot
ignore one another so well—

your eyes averted,
your hands stilled
on the table when I touch your thigh

after you've asked if we can heal,
like it's one thing,
something to wish for or expect:

a dawn on another shore
of this ever-turning world,
the chance to cross the river's thin ice
already overburdened with snow.

Flood Line

When you are gone like this,
days becoming months,
tulips blooming and then pears
growing heavy on their stems,
I find myself wanting
other men to press
their bodies against mine.

I imagine them leaning against me slightly,
in an alley stained with afternoon light,
or under the terrace of a restaurant,
cigarette smoke heavy in the air,
and then walking away
into the brown city and its fog.

I tell myself: I want them only as bodies.
But this isn't true, I want something else.
Perhaps I want desire itself,
desire a memory of the future,
remaking me in its deep sleep.

The days become cold.
A bitter wind flails from the north.
The tin wind chime on the porch
glitters with sound, the sound
of pebbles falling from a palm
on to a shore full of pebbles.

You must be in the hospital tent now,
among soldiers sitting like birds in a broken clock.
I see you holding a chart,
listening the way you listen, a waiting,
a clearing within yourself a space
for the other person.

The wind chime shakes and huddles the air.
It collides against itself, it jostles
its own corners. It reaches
and reaches for something else.

When I was young I wanted
to be changed by choice,
not by circumstance. And now
I wonder if they are the same thing.

Before you left we walked
along the floodplain of the Missouri River.
Scouring rush tilted in the wind,
cottonwoods drooped like fallen houses.
The flood-line darkened the bottom halves
of all the trees, a mark so perfect
it made another horizon.

On Confessing My Symptoms to My Doctor

—on *The Pink Peach Tree* by Van Gogh

I.

I am a pink peach tree
kind as a night in spring,
dropping moons into your palms.

I've roosted in this asylum
for half a decade, a week,
maybe a collection of hours,
and I still cannot move
with movements that are my own.

I haven't been stayed by your anchors,
my roots are the breeze.

II.

Today I unfold into whiteness,
tomorrow I may drop red leaves
at your feet. This is only an imitation
of a terminus; I do not become corpse,
but mock its dryness, mock skin and marrow.

III.

Each blossom swells, sores I wrap in bandages
only to uncover them and find each still growing.
Grant me your shocks and quivers,
reverberations of a mind
peeling back on itself,
the angel-haired fire,
for I want to burn like an old barn in the night,
flames a bustle up my neck and out my eyes.

IV.

What do I think of when you say the word healthy?

I think of a tree falling down
because an axe swings into its side
over and over.

In my world an elm will fall on its back
for no reason.
Its foliage still shining, its trunk still strong,
it sings as it falls.

V.

A hierarchy establishes itself in every kingdom.

God placed man at the top
to use lesser creatures.

But what of lesser creatures
that are not useful?

VI.

Do you smell my flowering?
How extravagant I can be?

I am not a thing to be harvested.
Instead, you prune me,
decide which parts of me can be kept.

VII.

I do not envy your choices,
your cabinet of drugs,
your files of instructions
on who will live
how. Between man and tree
the tree will ghost the man.

VIII.

You have examined my tentacles, my octopus arms
that stretch and foretell futures. You cannot reach
my particular glow, the odd light
gummed up in the back of my throat.

The Pleasure of Strangers

Baby howls in the next room
but there are vistas here—
glossy lakes and blue pines
teacups amid small cakes, families

arranged in a line. Phone blinks
on the bedside table. Silence
is the hand full of blades
roaming my mind.

If I see you, you see me.

Lace camisole, frozen
smile, feet in the ocean,
these images stack like busted cars
up to the clouds.

My daughter's face presses
close to mine
I cannot smell her hair.
For this, should I be sorry?

My eyes are coins.

Fingers whirl in this heat.
There are no pictures
of my home, where a lion sleeps
in my living room. His purr

is no tremble of fur against my hand—
it's the shuddering of his organs
as I curl in his belly,
safe, warm, blind.

Stillborn

"But howsoever, they dye like rotten sheepe noe man dies,
but he is as full of maggots as he can hould. They rott above ground."
                    —John Baldwin, a letter from Virginia, 1623

I, too, have taken root,
like a sore vessel unaccustomed
to the sea.

Last night I found a stillborn
swaddled within the branches
of a cherry tree.

It is spring so the white blossoms
scent the skin, making people
who hurry by my home
think it is just another flower.
However, in the moonlight
the babe's skin is too silver
against the white to think this,
the silver saying *never was*
and the white saying *only for a time.*

I cannot pull my roots out,
not even with my teeth
in the ground.

Origin Story

Last Sunday you told me how at midnight thirteen years ago,
you looked out at the thin layer of snow
glazing our acreage and heard a voice telling you
to stay with my father, to not
pack us three children into the cold car
and drive away that night.

Now, on this restaurant patio, rain glazes the railing
and a chokecherry tree grows,
buzzing in the dull light of a streetlamp,
its leaves yellow eyes in the night,
each branch its own animal with its own hungers.
I lift my face to smell that famous scent of rain,
all green and growth, all vines and hidden
gardens, and find none,
find only the sounds

of a passing car and a waiter collecting silverware
in his palm from the next table. There have been moments
when I felt chained by love's senseless devotion—
its sweat and blood, its gravity,
its crowding midnight hours—
and I blamed you for the sacrifices
you have made in my name.

In the only photograph I have of you as a young woman
you are gazing out the window of a barn,
sitting on a haystack, your white blouse delicate,
expanding in the breeze like a lung,
your curly dark hair painting light purple shadows
on your thin shoulders.

What is our common heritage
but Mary, looking up at the angel like a luminescent fool,

with no questions, her face blank as a bell that is rung and rung, metal against metal,

her face set like flint,
her eyes the unvanquished birds
that rise at dawn above the tree line,
their hollow bones lifted on the wind.

That Summer We Knew Each Other

Almost every weekend that summer,
you would join me on the porch at dusk.
As the night wore on we could see a raccoon
or possum stalking past, nothing visible
but its eyes and the silhouette of fur.

We are the sum of our parts, you would say.
Or, *I am not living, only existing.*

Words nothing like your flannel shirt,
or the glow of the streetlights,
or the thick scent of pine trees.

That August two hard rains fell.
Before and after heat hung in the air
like claws stuck in prey and steam caught in my throat.

I heard yesterday that you got a job
with a logging company up north.
That you don't speak to many people.
You read books, smoke, sit on your porch at night.

Once that August I opened your cedar box
to reach for a cigar and when I looked up
you were watching me.

Your look reminded me of a photo
I saw earlier that summer in a psychiatric museum.
The man was chained to a wall with an iron ring
around his neck, his feet bound with cloth.

An hour before the photo he may have been spun in a cage
or shaken or kicked or doused with water,

and still he remained tucked away.
He stared at the camera with his deep-set eyes

Please, interfere with me.

.

Travels in the Automobile

American road with its smooth asphalt,
a river running through town,
a way of sailing,
of moving for so long it becomes a kind of stillness.

They have been driving for four days,
nowhere, for no reason.
She stands alongside the road
in her wool coat, one hand holding a coffee mug,
the other hand nudging hair from her face,
telephone poles strung along the asphalt,
blurry in the distance, as though seen through a camera lens
that focuses only on what is near and present.

She is smiling, gap between her teeth
just barely visible, rust red of the wool
making her skin turn pale and translucent
in the autumn dawn.

Each movement they made,
is a calling out to one another in the night,
touching each other with their voices, with their tongues.

In tall grass he asks her how long
will it last, how long
will they lie on the earth
as they do now, her turned to him,
him gazing at the sky, picking
the tips off buffalo grass

how long will the metal car
sail along the asphalt, wind in her long hair,
him smelling her, smelling the lilacs
by the side of the road until

this kind of fire
has to burn out,
one of these hours,
on one of these roads.

Death Drive

I.

My skeleton is no set of bones
but a hunger I've buried.
A yearning for a god
with the mind of the moon,
a radiant string of revolutions.

I have organized my days badly,
spent hours like dimes in a cheap casino.
Even the stars are restless, wincing above
the little houses tucked in their yards.

II.

I am searching for a burial ground,
a place to stay awhile.
Each god remains a stranger,
except you. Take me home,
where a tulip grows in December,
where a rock floats in a dark lake.

Where is my life instinct,
purring like a kitten,
waiting to be stroked,
that erotic buzz in the veins,
unfolding, stretching toward the sun?

III.

I have an arrow for a soul
and the body of a crow,
a rising, a traveling,

that hums like a river
and can't be cleaned.

I've visited many gods' houses and nearly escaped
with a thing or two. A wood candlestick,
an embroidered tablecloth, but no jewel

between the lips of a stranger
that I could see.
Until you, no unexpected panderer
feeding me a mountain
from the palm of one's hand.

Never mind that it's a mountain of ash.
It tastes like honeysuckle
pulled through the flower's heart.

II.

To a Stranger

Forgive me, I have not said
what is on my heart

which is:
I'm sorry that when the rain fell
among the red roofs
of the Douro Valley
between palm trees
on a cobblestone street

I did not offer you
my umbrella,
dark-eyed girl in a blue dress,
damp and tired

with no need for me or another
but still wanting
like us all.

A Well-Regulated Society

—on *Sorrow* by Vincent van Gogh, drawing of Sien Hoornik

"If our society were pure and well regulated, yes, then they would be seducers;
but now, in my opinion, one may often consider them more as sisters of charity."
—Vincent van Gogh

There is no room for you at the inn.
Or in the stable, for that matter,
where horses break the air with their woolen breaths
and shuffle in the mud.

When you were a child at the orphanage
a nun wore a pouch of coins at her waist
and it rattled like music when she walked.

Mornings, you wake under a bridge or behind a shed.
Stone on bone, pressed cheek to cheek in your sleep.
The walnut tree on the hill, the rough grass under you,
carve their lines of bark and blade
into your skin beside a fallen wood fence.

At the seashore you watch sky and sea merge,
the horizon blur. You are pregnant with your second child.
When the tide recedes
it leaves small bodies in the sand,
a shell, kelp, a rotten log.
Unlike water they stay still.

You are coral with no tentacles.
Men slide right off when finished with their anchor,
their brief respite.
Is it grace to give someone all
they want and nothing more?

You smoke a cigar in front of the fire.
Peel potatoes. Mend a bonnet.

These things fill hours, but your sorrow—
it is a bone in your body that connects to the others,
allows the skeleton to work.

You pose for him and you create edges, your body speaks its shape.
Rock and flesh, little else. A portrait made still life,
your body an apple on a table.

During dinner he cuts your daughter's food into small portions for her.
You cannot look him in the eye.
Your daughter plays with beads on the wood floor.
She touches one and it rolls like a galloping wild animal
out of the room, out of sight,
as though it has been reborn
into a life we cannot see,
and have no reason to believe in.

Chorus of the Underground Sea

Beneath my feet my ancestors stir,
their fins move soundlessly in water that haunts
all I wanted and never had, for I have disappointed
the depths, have fallen short of its measures.
Still, that water irrigates my crops
and makes my children grow tall.

Their songs do not sing me to my death
but to the boundary beyond it, where dusk
does not darken the seabed plains and plateaus,
where my ancestors cast no shadows
on the brittle stars below them. They tell me

*There are dreams in your mouth
but your mouth is sewn shut.*

My deathbed confession will be to the women
under me who turned over and over,
bubbles in their hair, turquoise water in their ears,
and how I thought so little of them.
I thought only of my daily bread and it weakened me.

Rest, they will say, *The earth is our tombstone.*
And I will rest
before I enter your body in the water you drink,

I will bless your bones
before I call them home.

Abandoned Farmhouse

We lost ourselves in saffron hills
looking for water. Surrounded
by cottonwoods and tall grass

the house was as unexpected
as a tender eglantine,
impossible to dry and keep.

That dusty road where you touched
my hair remembers
nerves taking flight,

the cranes overhead
ascending and ascending until transfigured
to air and song.

I became to myself a land of want.
Gone now,
farther than a possible migration,

you still frighten me with the snow owls
in the attic of the collapsing house,
with their shifting feet and fluffed

alabaster feathers, their onyx eyes
black pearls sitting in a white oyster shell.

Wind Chime

You have not written me in weeks
and I do not know if you will be returning
home. If you do return home,
even then you will be gone,
your eyes will be full of secret places
I cannot reach, the black space
in a buffalo's eyes,
after it has fallen to the ground.

Last we spoke you described
the desert full of sheep, herded by a military truck,
having been smuggled across the Syria-Iraq border.
Their bleats called out to you in the distance,
between gunfire, when you're mopping blood
from the linoleum of the emergency room floor.

A patch of mushrooms grows in the front yard now.
Some days, before work, I listen and watch
the wind chime that hangs off the front porch.
It is made of tin stars and moons, like cheap jewelry
or trinkets one buys in tourist shops.

Songbirds sing in the cherry blossom tree all day.
I try to imagine them like your sheep—
imagine that they are calling out to me,
my own chorus, a music to measure my life.
But they go on singing as though I cannot hear them,
as though I am not here.

Now, I see that one of the crescent moons
has fallen from the wind chime
into the branches of the bushes.
It is caught and held,
a halted, falling star.

For Matthew

Nothing like your mask to make me silly
with fright. As though you could be any old scarecrow,
in black boots, a plaid shirt, with my wood pipe
stuck in the rip of your mouth. That Halloween
before you were seventeen you needled me
with a feather, my hair rising, the ears of a wolf
awakened by the scent of prey or predator,
at that ghost touch, that touch
there after it had left. My gingham dress
right above my black oxfords
and the paper sack with the three slits hanging over my head,
baring what I wanted, not unlike honesty.
How I grew tired of your gold key to unlock my skull
so it would split open like a halved pumpkin for its seeds.
We stood in the field, square shouldered
as soldiers for a photograph, dry leaves buzzing under our shoes,
shattered and numerous. I could always see you holding a yellow broom
as though to sweep me up into neat little piles.
How to endure the half sight of being seen?
A bell knelled over the field and we scurried to the bonfire,
its flames jumping up in the rhythm of sound and echo,
shadow and self, the never gone or here.

Flea Market in Brownsville, NE

The old man sits behind his booth
in denim and plaid, a wad of tobacco
in the pocket of his cheek.

He nods at the people who pass
his table, heavy with his handmade clocks
and his wife's crocheted doilies.

A week before, his granddaughter
died of eclampsia, the seizure catching
her arms and legs, twisting her wrists,
pulling her head back, pulse

in her neck thudding, then slowing.
He sits and waits. His heart ticks.
For the first time in thirty years

he cannot remember a face
after it passes him by.
The faces are things, foreign things,

objects on another person's table.
And he also—an object on a chair—
his skin the tin of a fishing box, rusted,

still holding its tackle and bait.
At her service he watched the thrashing
fires of votive candles.

He knows the world shakes
when you leave it. Even the branch
quivers when a bird takes flight.

Psychoanalysis of Fire

I.

When I was a child, my house caught fire in the night. Once it had gone out, everything was soft as a piece of spoiled fruit. This was how I learned to give way, to allow myself to be consumed.

II.

When my lover left me I stared hard at the candle's flame flickering above our kitchen table. It had its own spirit and I put on that spirit like an old coat hidden in the back of the closet. I was extinguished and reanimated. I can be the dark side of fire, the smoke that lingers and then dissipates.

III.

A wildfire spreads under a gray sky. The trees close as they hide smaller selves within until they can no longer be found. The marsh water mirrors birds. Their dark shapes rise in the sky and rise in the water, but they disappear at the shore, swallowed by their own need to escape.

III.

Marriage

Marriage is entirely too long.
Even a moment of marriage
would be too long,
the splitting of self,
the boundary between us made permeable

by oath and blood. I feel you in my blood
even now, how you inhabit me
in ways I never requested.

I smell you, I taste you,
but I can never touch you,
cannot cup you in my palms,
keep you containable, something
I can put my finger on.
Which is what I want.

Our children with their milk skin
and milk bones, made of my body,
soldered with my breath, their tiny joints
metal of my mouth,

even they sense
the space between us

and they mourn it.
What would it be to be whole,
to be one, to be a field of lilies,
and not just a petal,
already broke free and loose in the wind.

You evade me still.
I've hungered for you before time,

before the stars split atoms
and combed darkness
like a child's fingers
reaching for warmth in the night.

Peasant Girl

—on the painting by Van Gogh

Measles, Tuberculosis, Cholera,
Diphtheria, Smallpox, Typhus—
so many names to plague a body.
And yet none of them
are the reason you sit so strangely,
so ill at ease. Your bonnet
and apron hum with the same tone
of the wheat field. Your dress
sings the same blue as your eyes,
which stare out into the distance,
looking at nothing, wanting to see nothing.

You have taken the years given to you
and let them grow like sunflowers in the field,
indistinguishable, all turned toward the sun.
These years are now fossils above ground.

The poppies can be seen in your cheeks,
as though you are mirrored by your surroundings,
as though you yourself could be made like wheat
into many different things,
with different names.

Depression

"Depression is a practice."
—*American Handbook of Psychiatry*, 1874

And oh, have I practiced.
I have practiced with my thumbs and tongue,
my blinking in the morning,
and my breathing at night,
I have practiced in each thought,
formed and nurtured it like a child
in the palm of my hand,
pinched it till it blisters,
a blanched doll, boiling in a pot.

My wanton skeleton mimics
your muscles, their clenching and releasing.
I, too, take days off.
On those days I don't count the ways I've failed.

On days out of the hospital
my ritual is two cups of coffee,
a vigil at the kitchen window.
Two blackbirds stand on the telephone wire.
They do not speak; they step over electricity.

This asylum has a room with four bathtubs
and I'm dropped in ice cold water,
surprise the medication of the day,
the surprise supposedly:
your body can feel greater pain than your brain.

Numb, but certainly no real winter.
I censor myself before your altar,
shelter in the liquor
of reserved, composed, quiet.
I've not found their addiction,
though their virtues are praised.

I am immune to their cocoon.
The spoons with liquid that fill my mouth,
pour into another vessel.
I have practiced and mastered my own healing,
sitting in a room,
my mind licking me clean.

To a Childhood Neighbor

Remember the tree down by the river
with the swing and wood fort in its branches,
and how your brother saved me from drowning that summer
when I sank with the raft

limbs in the water
he and I a current of bones.
When we were thirteen
you and I found a beaver's skeleton
in the bank

small and delicate
shrunken like a crescent moon
and you wanted its teeth
to hide in your drawer

a treasure like anything else
that has been threatened and still remains.
Remember our walks home in the snow
after feeding the neighbor's horses.
Between pines and how we thought we knew what we wanted
hands in pockets
stars pearls on an iron sheet.

I am not the great love
of your life and you are not mine.
Yet you persist in me, occasionally you rise up,
your freckles in the sunlight,
the perfect scar on your jaw
from a stray fishing hook.

That next August you stole a stalk
of my mother's rhubarb
and I chased you to the river

chose to fold my torso
between the barbed wires of a farmer's fence
rather than leap over it

hoped I wouldn't catch you.

Dawes County, Nebraska

Silence buzzes like a fever over the prairie.
A tomcat lies on the porch, in the clear light
of the moon. Stars ache with their blurred
edges, letting time burn like a buffalo's skeleton
in the sun. Because I cannot awake
with a single bright eye in my bones
I have unraveled within my own hands,
a mass of knotted threads. My failure
is hoarfrost over my bones. I stumble
against the chairs I sit on and the door handles I clasp.
These objects are comforting with their firm bodies.
I have always wanted to be such a thing,
with its corners all confidence.
For them, death is not failure, but time spent.

I remember you stood at the edge
of the badlands, saying words like hope, but the sky
and grass, moving in reflections of one another unaligned,
emphasized the absurdity.
Maybe in a house I could believe you, maybe in a school or a church,
but not there, where if we placed our toes beyond
the ridge of the prairie we dropped into impermanence.
I felt you had a god in your mind you could match
with words, but I didn't know how to interpret
all the movement, the running clouds,
the soil that would crumble under my hand.

Elegy

Autumn leaves drift in my veins
and go still. I am a house
in which every door has been shut,
every window shuttered.

Last night I had a dream of giving you
myself as a pocket watch you could rub
between your fingers when standing in the cold
waiting for a train to arrive and take you home.

Baghdad, Euphrates River, Ramadi.
A sheet of metal leaning against a palm tree.
Concrete caved in, crumbling in a steep slope,
an arm, a smashed head, visible between rocks.

My desires, the ones I have not aborted,
passions I have carefully selected, line up before me
as little children awaiting their bedtime medicine.
When you died last week I told myself
I no longer chose you, and yet here you are,
your mouth waiting for the teaspoon of syrup,
and I cannot refuse you.

Down the street a small boy's shoes
echo on the cobblestones. He cries
in a thin voice for his mother.
She is buying day-old bread from the baker,
picking change at her palm. I do not have
many clear moments like this, standing at the window,
playing the observer. It makes the world seem
made of glass, everyone's intents laid out
like nightclothes on a bed.

Yesterday, I cleared dead leaves
from the lawn. Goats scampered up the hillside,

turned their thin heads to watch me.
They moved as if there is no time and space,
just rocks, dry grass, a faint smell of rotting apples.

I need you to be my Pastoral.
Not a grassy field with a horse grazing nearby
and sunflowers turned toward light,
but a river that is home in its every current.
I need it to be all brambles, animal scent,
bodies in the dirt to birth me again
and again, us always parallel,
until we rub into transparency.

Train Station in Amsterdam

I watch the train halt before
it reaches the metal stoppers.
And she is here with me, haunting me
in this station, with the way she stopped
just short of death.

Trauma service in fourth year medical school.
Vehicle collision with drunk driver.
Life support until after organ donation.

The body can be cruel, denying what we want,
always denying a sense of completion
or arrival, always asking for more.

She lay still and silent on the bed.
She moved through me like a woman
opening a house to fresh air,
walking into each room,
lifting the windows,
pulling back the drapes.

As a child I wanted that extra moment
on the high dive, a bit of clear space
to consider my collision from air to water.
The longer I stood the more it took and did not return.

In those gaps of space between here and there
I've become a room for prayer.

Fairy Tale for My Unborn Child

While walking in the riverbed behind our house I discover a village, half hidden in tall grass that reaches the windows of cottages. A sign reads: no one in this town is afraid to die.

I hear children's songs; see them lined in one row wearing their Sunday best; black trousers on the boys, navy dresses on the girls. This is a town with pastries on the baker's windowsill, set in small boxes tied with yellow ribbon, and a market where a man butchers chickens, with the blood right there next to the flower shop, the daffodils bright and inviting.

The fabric store holds rolls of velvet, chiffon, and brocade, where dark-haired girls stick pins into fabric mannequins. Their gray wool dresses darken their eyes in the November dusk, when closing shop they bend and blow out the last candle on the windowsill.

Beside a thatch-roofed cottage, an ax balances against a tree trunk. The stained glass in the cathedral are a multitude of burning eyes, lit aflame by the sun. Children line up and sing among the tombstones. Each child's voice burns with the same moon, an open mouth, a wide, untreated wound.

Beyond them stands a field of wildflowers. Each meadow is an untended cemetery, each bird song a herald, each new birth a temptation for curses— too much beauty, too much light, for any one sky.

IV.

Before World

It's too much and too little—
the tiny hand in your palm,
skin not even the color of skin,
some color before they become human,
still half part of that before world
you cannot even dream of.

Too much, like sunshine,
you squinting and not able to see
when you drive home at the wrong
time. Them taking you always outside time,
that moment their mouth first opened
outside you,
new animal's holy howl
in a forest with no name.

Too little, even in your heart,
which cannot hold their iris
like a glass of water, pure
as some glacier
already melted to memory.

Mademoiselle Ravoux

—on the painting by Van Gogh

The sunflowers grow taller this year.
They nearly touch the sun. I climb a ladder
and cut their heads off. I settle into time
and the ways it betrays me.

The old canal tastes everything,
but especially skin. It laps up against legs
in its waters, it splashes the arms of men
untying ropes of boats.

I have seen time drifting past me,
in its mosaic pieces, flowing like a current
of broken glass. It is more blue than the sky
the sunflowers live in, more blue than the canal,
an entirely new blue of voice and throat,
of a mouth full of teeth.

I am submerged in this current,
I bite down on this life,
clench it like a wolf at a carcass
in winter, unaware this bone
is not the meat I hunger for.

A Mother's Birth, 1897

I am my mother's empty basket, her cracked
bottle of rum, the door left an inch open
with a draft drifting through.

These are the chills in my pockets
full of candy, my cheeks surprisingly not
rosy. Her body trembles, a thin-boned deer.

I have emerged cold and white
as a porcelain figure spinning in a music box.
Mother does not weep but stares with a new white,

a luminous rage. I have electrified her,
annulled her fingers and toes,
combed right up to her scalp

and peddled away her husband's flannel,
foxglove under the window, the railroad
junction her father laid one mile

from this cabin. I am a ladder
with no place to get off at the top.
It is my body that strikes her pendulum into motion

until she grips me so tight my bones moan.
Days later, she will barter for these moments
between the wrought iron bedposts, the blood

still hot between her thighs and a filament
of smoke caught in the chimney,
a thin body hung to dry.

Assistens Cemetery, Copenhagen

We spent over an hour looking
for Kierkegaard's grave. It wasn't far,
but we kept taking wrong turns,

kept walking over the same paths and forgot
we'd been there before. Among a cluster of family graves,
surrounded by a black iron wrought fence,

we saw a stone statue of a woman
with a spider web draped over her face
in a veil. Iridescent in the rain,

the cobweb's silk finer than an eyelash,
the veil both hiding and revealing
her face at the same time.

You had said, *sometimes, I want to know what
it's all for,* our heels soft on the stones,
our breath almost visible before our faces.

You said *want*, but I felt you meant *need*.
A sort of prerequisite to continue on,
a survival that needs a different end.

Today I cycled through a national park,
between cedar trees, through sand dunes,
among grasslands, and kept seeing us

lost among the graves, trying to find our way.
I stopped at a marsh, where the water and wet grass
filled the air with its woody scent, not quite fertile,

and not yet dead. In a shallow nook a wildflower grew,
its whole body underwater but the head,
a yellow blossom, floating on the surface.

Squatters in a Dead Woman's Tenement

German Immigrants, New York City, 1885

I.

The dead woman lies on a mattress Mother has pulled to the corner of the room. Mother keeps smiling, despite the rats and one window without glass. She says our lives are waiting to be cut open from the black willow tree.

My sister says it was likely a lover who left the woman with purple blooming across her face. Herta wants an American boy to buy her ribbons. Her story will be better than Mother's, or grandmother's, she says, who married farmers and never had more than two pairs of shoes. Holding her back straight, Herta waits, crossing her ankles so that her black laced-up boots are held out at appealing angles.

II.

Each morning Father descends a shaking staircase to reach the docks and heave coal, his hands black and limp when he returns to the tenement. I sew knickerbockers by candlelight with Herta. When I run to the bakery, I pause in front of the oven and remember the warmth of our old cellar and the rows of cabbage.

Returning to the tenement, I pass a blonde-haired girl who is curled in a threadbare blanket. Men walk by with clean jackets, jackets made with wool so thick I stop and stare until I move on, past more tall brick buildings that hover between clouds.

Father buys a cigar and lights it while fish fries over the fire. Mother's chrysanthemum on the windowsill heaves its red through the smoke like a wagon that hasn't arrived, like a boat that doesn't bother landing on a shore gray and dirtied as a blanket in an alley.

III.

Orange light from the kerosene lamp shudders over the ash gray walls. The stench from the body expands, makes my skull vibrate, my vision blur.

Mother grows weary of watching the skin thin until it takes on the color of bone. The body is a painting we have stepped into. No matter how we move, where we sit in the room, it holds us, a portrait in a frame. Bugs crawl in and out of her as though she were made of many doors.

We speak in whispers. When Mother weeps she goes out into the hallway. The woman doesn't seem dead, if dead means gone.

A crow dives off our windowsill and is lifted on the wind, a black boat in clear water, no struggle in its still, sailing body.

IV.

Before sunrise my parents carry the body to the street and leave it resting on the curb, hoping she will be too nameless to be recognized. When sunlight drifts over her the bruises on her face become petals reaching for the sky.

She deserves songs from the old world, but here only a flock of pigeons surround her. They settle around her body as though she held invisible branches, as though she were a tree felled to build another's house.

Searching for a Pup Born Outside
on a Winter Evening

In the forest behind our house
time and the cold was a blanket over him,
smothering him into oblivion,
its steady pressure a hand closing his eyes.

Before we found him, I feared he'd fade like smoke,
his edges dissolving
as though he'd never been. The first word
of a sentence, erased.

Niobrara River Valley

Four years ago cancer swept up my brother, broke
him into pieces under his skin, leaving
our parents' house in my name.
So I moved home to the plains in the high heat
of summer, the Honey locust and Cottonwood
blocking the wind on the front walk,
blooming a valley of stillness and sweat.

I've given time in this life, brushed it into the floor as I swept,
wrung it into a rag by the kitchen sink.
I've spent myself against such surfaces.
During most of it I wasn't there.

One winter, pronghorns watched me with their black eyes
as though they recognized me, could name
me in the arch of their necks.
I hurried across the field.
Now that I am counting my last days
I think of them, how on a morning walk
in the grasslands they would stop
with one hoof raised and watch
my passing. That day the sky hung white as frost,
my flesh lost its porcelain
to a wash of denim blue spreading in thin veins.
A female stood so still
I felt her gaze like a rope extended I didn't know how to clutch.
Survival has always seemed a mean thing to me.
But she held time like a peacock's wing,
brushing the air with rows of eyes, unblinking.
To live and to die were never such opposites
as on that day, in the frozen,
broken grass.

Painting Cypress Trees in Northern Louisiana

Dried from winter, bark shrivels
like the discarded skin of a copperhead.
Dirt and water huddle tree roots.

These trees do not mimic your brazen look,
your eyes in Indian ink,
delicate splashes on canvas.

Too harmonious a rhythm,
they stand grave and limp
as my mother's hands on Sundays.

You ghostwrite my work;
any subject does. Even these trees do,
where behind the cattails
a baby alligator floats, his snout

trained on blood. Once,
balanced on a stool,
black hair on one side of your neck,

you solicited cobalt blue
to your temples, where there was none.
You were full of vengeance,

with perfect shadows between your bones.
In the filtered light through the window
your skin was a mosaic

only you could assemble.
Before the underpainting dries
I blend wet on wet,

hurry after the corded texture
of bark, but it too wants revenge,
says it will be seen its own way.

A Witch's Lament

Electric wine on my sleeve, I wobble
on the tiles. Pots of ragweed and bamboo,
a jar of teeth, a bucket of stew, line my kitchen counter.
My lover has left, grown tired of me,
did all but say: you are not the woman I want.

I spin, I wring, I jazz across the floor,
a tycoon of wills. I buzz bright blue—
a fly with two great eyes.
My cottage stands crooked
in the forest, a man with a broken
knee, and its stones blink and blink
and still cannot see
through the darkness of these early
morning hours.

I've thumbed
through all my potions and for this,
none will do.

None will summon back up who I imagined myself to be.
She evaporated, a shadow soaked up by the sun.

Each time he sank into me, a ship falling
into the deep blue sea,
my inner parts rose, rearranged, tide sucked in
then spilled out. I floated in an inner black,
suspended, empty, no magnetic fields, no push and pull,
no boundaries
between myself and all else.

My houseplants rot from too much water,
the scent of decomposition warms the room like fur.
Death wish in neither angel nor animal.

I'll buy an orchid today, that corpse curl,
that thin neck I've envied for so long.
I'll eat the petals, one by one, each swallow

my birth, until I too,
will bloom the deep burgundy,
the absent tumbleweed.

V.

Becoming

I've become each and every thing
at one time or another.
Shutters silently sitting on either side
of a window. A gas leak
waiting to burst into flames in a basement.
Stones stacked into a wall
monochromatic and textured as old teeth.

Each has been my unraveling
and my clawing for a place.
Spool of red thread fallen from a table.

They've even been small deaths.
The movement of a rocking horse
after someone has left it, the anxious slowing,
the hobbling toward stillness,
it being not a tree or a horse,
but nicely carved wood
that is no longer breathing.

All Good Things

—on *Head of a Prostitute* by Van Gogh

All good things come to those who submit
madame said, reclining beneath a sycamore tree.
Break me softly, lest I remain unlit.

Out my window a thousand dragonflies emit
a light beyond measure or boundary.
All good things come to those who submit

I hear in my head when I'm rubbed with grit.
I'm as a useful as a candlestick or chimney.
Break me softly, lest I remain unlit.

I swallow without breathing, a gill slit
caught in air, instead of the deep blue sea.
Remind me good things come to all who submit.

Any disease will help me remember I am unfit.
Tell me why even the blackbird is not free.
It may break me softly, till I become unlit.

Today the sun rose with no light in it,
only a cold song that sang darkly,
no one knows what comes to those who submit.
This breaks me softly, until I remain unlit.

For the Boy Across the Street Who Sets Out His Grandmother's Trash

My hope is that you'll know misfortune sharp and early
in a containable way. Not like my friend,
recently divorced and unemployed, who lines his kitchen
now with empty liquor bottles.
Not like our neighbor who saw his friend
shot to death in the park just south of us.

The daffodils won't come up this spring
because it's been falsely warm. They need
steady thawing.

When you set the trash can by the drive
you kept your head down and aligned
it just so, edging the street, before
you got on your bike to join the other children.

My hope is that you'll remember this—
the care you've given small things,
and that later, years later,
the small things will begin giving back.

After the Funeral

I set the head of a magnolia blossom
on the pond's still surface.

Ivory in the sunlight, the blossom
is a photograph of a dead face.
I would hang it on my wall
so it could watch everything
and know the stillness—

mornings in the kitchen
when dawn and I do not move,
but breathe into the vague repeating,
the coffee and newspaper.

Uncle

When I thanked you for the book
you gave me on my sixth
birthday you were embarrassed

and took a long gulp of beer.
On car rides I would read
it and think of you,

while you slept with a gun
under your pillow and woke up
screaming out the window.

At a family picnic you sat outside
smoking a tobacco pipe,
laughter from your throat

hard as German syllables,
and your hands shook from the image
of so many people moving across the lawn.

It was so slow, your leaving.
At first we didn't notice,
but then, you couldn't put your shoes

on the right feet, and this,
this meant you weren't coming back
to us with your swearing

and diffident gift giving,
your stubbornness and acid humor,
your eyes veined with their own thunderbolts.

In the end, we were as scared
of you as you were. We took
Grandma out of her house

to get away from you and she wept
for her son, as you starved in your childhood
home, now dark and quiet.

On the china hutch sits a photo
of you when you were young,
standing on the scrubland

of Vietnam, watching
the camera through sunglasses.
A skinny, camouflaged boy.

Night in the Arctic Tundra, 1864

My husband should have returned by the second evening with or without a reindeer's carcass. My canoe breaks the water, a comb's tail parting black hair. I do not know whether I am searching for him or my own end. My blood knows, but will not say.

Before me a cave is winnowed in the base of the cliff by lapping water. Once inside I hold my lamp up to the cave walls. Etching of a female holding a child. A wolf. A snow owl. I find two skeletons—one adult, the other smaller; so small the skull fits in my palm like a cold teapot.

That night I awake to an owl's call, vibrating between the walls. It is asking who is left, counting, taking the names of those who remain. The next morning, I lay the bones in my canoe and push off into the bright light. One iceberg I pass looks like my own face, with my features rubbed off.

My husband will be an etching by my own hand; he will not be reduced to surf on an opposite shore. Strangers may carry us during our last journey and this must be enough. I drop each bone into the sea. The water swallows it eagerly, as though it has been waiting all this time for every lost body to return to it.

At the Veteran's Hospital

"Everything we travel through is thorny and rough. There is no chance to save your clothes."
—Elizabeth Smith, traveler on Oregon trail, 1845

Father's hospital gown lies on the bed.
Skin hangs loose on his hands
and creases at joints like crumpled silk.
Both hands shake and fumble with the suspender buckle
at the top of his jeans, a silver clasp
glinting in florescent lights.
He already managed the plaid shirt
with pearl snap buttons and the coffee-colored cowboy boots.

Ready to haul hay, ready to ride one of the horses
to the south pasture. Eighteen years ago
he crushed the skulls of my kittens in the barn.
Too many, he had said.
I buried their bodies in the backyard,
but not deep enough, the coyotes still dug them up,
left bloody fur scattered about the forest behind our house.

Hospital bills pile on Mother's kitchen counter.
Insurance, she says, her eyes darting,
not frozen like a deer's, but wild,
still full of hope, looking for a way out.
Some animals know their end,
some don't.

During our first hunting lesson
I couldn't see the doe,
her coat blended into elms and maples.
A blue moon in a blue sky.
After the bullet lodged in her chest
and I knelt beside her, my first,
I saw she was finally naked.
After we gutted the deer, we hung

her in the barn. Her legs splayed
and her torso open like a wide red mouth,
her head jerked up by the wire,
stretching her graceful neck taut.
When father butchered her,
privilege, responsibility,
were his words, as his knife
separated hide from meat and bone.
The organs piled in the field,
her meat piled on the table,
her hide now a rug at our feet.
Her body now a string of bones.
If only he could divide his heart so neatly,
my mother once said.

Are you ready to go home? I ask him now.

He looks up at me, his eyes clouded,
focused on me, but not seeing me.
My hands are broke. He lifts the clasp
in his palm, holding it up to me
as a gift, or permission, or a request.

Thin Ghosts

On the floor of the forest his weight
makes my spine grind tiny basins in a line.
I discover how dirt

is indifferent as hands, how animals
can slip into silence
like the quiet of a sacred

ritual. Overhead,
I catch a raven watching us,
black eyes observing fate form

in the forked
movements. I tuck
the position of the sun

into my spinning cocoon,
note the trees' long lines.
My hand unrolls out of a fist,

and I find it blue and icy.
Memory is a bed
I lie in when awake.

It keeps everything dried
in tiny rows, the sounds
of the forest brittle and distant,

but real enough to clutch.
My thin ghosts
are reverent children.

Photo Shoot

I am underwater and smiling; white paint encompasses my left eye.
Cold, teal water shifts around me, fluid muscles bright on my burning
eyes. Soul needs exercise, too. A yellow cape floats
at each shoulder, two delicate angels. My striped stockings flash their lines
as I kick to keep from sinking further down, down, down

The photographer hunts for my elbows and knees. I move them at careful
angles; position my knees as soft flowers spreading petals, round as eyes
and just as open. I swallow water and it floods my lungs but this hardly matters.
I glisten, I glow.

Tulle around my waist lifts in thin clouds so that my arched spine is concealed.
Pink powder and black lines fall from my right eye so dark tears halt
on my cheek. I cannot breathe.
My burgundy hair suspends, spreads in a long lion's mane, making my skin
wildly beautiful, my hair awake as tiny animals surrounding their queen.

I do not know what to believe.
On all sides it is dark: a black, aloof forever. Space keeps going and going,
making me feel that I am not here. Ripples echo my skin when I rise to the surface.
Down the street a marching band is playing

Oh when the saints

VI.

Confession

In the night, when the streetlamps
glow in the dark water
of the canal, and yellow leaves
fall from trees on to the cobblestones,
I think not of what I have done,
but of what I have not done.

In the square past the wine shops
and delicatessen with cheese rolls
smug against the cold windowpane,
a man plays an accordion,
the notes low, mournful,
each song a Russian nesting doll
breaking in two to reveal
the same face, until you open
the last and all that's left is air.

I have failed every kind of love
there is and have taken my leave,
always in a foreign land,
among the same flowers,
among the same silent waters.

Rain and fog spread across the city.
I pass brick walls covered in vines,
an old clock tower where bells ring midnight,
and a dozen houses with red roofs,
lined along the street like packages
waiting to be opened.

I walk out of the city,
down a country lane
with green fields on either side

and sheep in the cold wet,
huddled among their own kind.

It is a little like the field
last April, where I stood in a meadow
of wildflowers, a woman
in a flowered dress, who has decided
that she doesn't know how to go home.

Interrupted Supper

—on *Still Life by* Jacob van Es

I am not here to tell you that death is simply relocation.
Yet this still life radiates movement,
a haunting of objects by those who left them.

Lemon rind curled on a silver plate.
Pomegranate hollowed like a waning moon.
I, too, have left a table unfinished.

When I left home for the first time
the scent of honeysuckle hung
in the air, a glass of water shook

when I stood up. Light and dust
bathed the orchard in a translucent veil.
Fallen apples rotted in the grass

and the rumble of a tractor
pushed across fields to where I stood
next to my car, holding my suitcase.

Birds stroked their feathers in the shadows
of pines and I balanced
between two worlds, as one dreaming of rain

while it rains outside on your windowpanes.
In every world, what the body needs is secondary.
I shed my silhouette on the gravel road

beside a cornfield. Maple trees lined the road
and the farthest trees faded in the fog, their branches
cobwebs, indistinct save a catch of light,

their disappearance measured,
as though when I left home I moved inside
the sort of frame where you go on and on.

August, 1942

Hours pass quickly,
short black lines
on the birch trees
outside our bedroom
window. I do not sleep
there anymore; I live
with a friend in town
because of rations on gas.
This is not

the only thing that has changed.
I type for a lawyer
during the day,
and knit scarves by thin
electrical lights at night.
I knit with blue yarn because it is your favorite.
Sometimes it is sky blue, navy blue,

or the gray-blue of your eyes
when shot quiet with love.
I do not drink coffee anymore
but sleep through still afternoons.
Sometimes, I want to keep
on sleeping.

Surely, by our house in the hills
all of the lilacs have stopped blooming
and begun to stoop
for it is nearly September
and the woolen air
follows me closely now.
Perhaps, by the time this letter
reaches you

the lilacs will be unfolding again,
the scent so thick it will creep
into the laundry and your beard,
its fragrance teeming
like fresh words
deep from your throat I have laid

my lips on, as if to feel
their forming, syllables
white and undying.

Grandmother

What came first were the dresses
made from chicken feed sacks,
the rough material smoothed by your young hands
on a table, early in the morning, or late
at night, perhaps by kerosene,
or by daylight swarming the open window
overlooking the farm. Later
came the cotton blouses, the polyester slacks,
the lace for my mother's wedding dress,
the rayon blend for my sewing lessons,
patterns tossed aside,
dotted chalk lines across fabric,
pins stuck in and out, tension knob twisted,
these all being things that were done,
your mind still silent to mine.
And yet, this is the way I have known you,
beyond our words,
words that are really secrets holding their shape,
birds that fall into formation and then,
upon nearing the ground, fall out.

In the Fire Before They Drift to Sleep

—on *Pollard Birches by* Van Gogh

Is it that we must first dream
of grace before we can see
it in our lives?

Is that why we draw silhouettes of struggle—
trunks knotted as arthritic hands,
branches tense and upright
as soldiers at command?

These trees stand as an old man who has outgrown the world
and now holds himself steady not by muscle, but will.

The shepherd with his flock of sheep
and the woman with a rake over her shoulder
walk heavy footed in the soil,
going to work, or coming home from work.
They shrink next to the trees,
they shelter in the long shadows.

Before them stretches dry grass, birches, sky,
a smattering of distant farm houses.
Before they return home
who will let them see
how the birches grow
like a child's bones,
imperceptible, impervious to gravity?

She cuts the soil, the sheep cluster
about his knees. In the evening
they will peel potatoes in candlelight,
sweep soot off the hearth.
There will be longing for change,
which means relief.

They will look for it in the morning weather,
in a stranger's face, in the fire
before they drift to sleep.

Asp & Venom

I.

Upstairs in the kitchen, a small girl
holds a viper straight against the table
so her father can slit its belly and drain the blood.
On assignment in this Vietnamese restaurant
I photograph the locals, ceramic dishes
painted in batik patterns, fires in the kitchen,
and bottles of rice wine in the basement

infused with snakes and lizards and snake eggs.
The menu reads: snake blood vodka, snake heart shot,
cures for pain, supplements for virility.
Lizards lie vertically, feet tucked
at the bottom of the glass, throat to throat,
a bracelet strung tight. Snakes coil
like baskets in their jars and eggs sit heavy
in their shells, a couple dozen stones
with still hearts.

II.

That apothecary of bodies remains with me,
as I sit next to my husband
quiet in his bed, chemo in his veins,
and I know I'll take anything—

a church steeple standing between stars,
holy water and incense, the laying of hands,

or vials of medicine, white hospital corridors,
charts and monitors, a constellation of signs,

or that cobra in his glass bottle,
hood flexed wide, body risen like a ghost,

I'll take anything. That he may continue
on, in a time and place away from me,
is a comfort like a boarded up window,
a train lying on its side in the grass.

Northern Montana

The moose stands between the moon
and a redwood tree, swallowing leaves.
Its eyes are flightless ravens.

If I were to touch its body
I'm certain it would be like stone or water,
some force, some element
I can touch and touch, and still not know.
Its face is blank as a skull,
a room that has been emptied.

I have seen death generate movement—
dirt tossed, flowers laid,
again and again a mourner kneeling before stone.

But not here.
Below this dirt trail, behind the elderberry
and dogwood, a river flows.
And if I were to fall among the rocks and water,
the moose would watch,
those eyes would not blink,
and it would see an erasing both familiar and distant,
leaf stuck in its throat,
soon washed away.

The Potato Eaters

—on the painting by Van Gogh

And so it is, potatoes and coffee,
dim light of the lantern,
pouring of the drink,
holding of the cup.

Their table is their altar.
Beyond their hut the old canal flows by,
rich in its elegance, in its green sophistication,
outliving us all.

Not a spirit, but an older
kind of body, its mind
a corporeal pleasure, lovely as a lady
reclining on a chaise lounge.

The potato eaters' faces are not
yellow ochre, burnt sienna, raw umber.
With those hands they have tilled the field,
swept the floors, forked the hay.

And so it is, dust unto dust,
yet they remain,
bodies in the dark, ghosts
of food and fields, unforsaken.

Estrangement

Does it matter that the same man
held us on a farm in southern Illinois
forty years ago, the sun a broken compass,
bleaching the sky white until darkness
came and tamped down our expectations?

That night brought mosquitoes and the birdcall
of surprise and attack, our breathing level as we listened,
bedcovers pulled up to our chins. I don't know that it matters

that we sat in the same doorway of a corn silo,
legs dangling like fish from our brothers' fishing poles,
hope and hunger unquenched and the steer
in the field beyond a mass of roaring blood and muscle,

look, look at him,
you'd only see red.

Our bodies are not our own, nor our ancestors.
They say the same blood flows in your veins and mine,
but I've swallowed different bees than you;
they swarm me,

stitch me together with honey,
circle inside me because they haven't yet stung
their way into death,
haven't asked the name
of the queen they're dying for.

A Fable

Under the leaves of a dogwood
forget-me-nots unfurl.

In my village, everyone knows I've become a miniature person.
I denied it until my sister took me to a lake
and pointed into it. There, with my head
reaching her waist, I saw how my actions have made me,

days of hauling water from the well,
building a fire at the hearth,
buying pork from the butcher.

All the sounds of the meadow
snapped shut, the sun's heat lifted from my back

and I remained in this form until
I traveled up the mountain
to the witch doctor and requested a new body.

When she finished my bones were splintered
and still small. I wanted to know when they'd grow.
The healing is part of the making, she said.

Now I lie in a cave, listen to the black sounds
of the forest, an owl's flight, water lapping
a bank. Like night, I can close myself away and wait.

It is not only the gods who go from death
to life and back again
in seasons. In all my graves
I have pulled the flowers down by their roots.

With these yellow brushes
I paint a mud door fragrant as birth.

ACKNOWLEDGMENTS

I am grateful to the following publications where these poems appeared, sometimes in earlier versions or under different titles:

Contrary Magazine, Coffin Bell, Thimble Magazine, Rust + Moth, Nightingale & Sparrow, Ghost City Review, Gingerbread House, Maryland Literary Review, Nebraska Poetry Anthology, War, Literature and the Arts, Literary Bohemian, Midwest Quarterly, Menacing Hedge Anthology, Briar Cliff Review, Stone Highway Review, Sow's Ear Review, Plainsongs, Prairie Schooner, Ekphrasis, South Dakota Review, Ellipsis, Platte Valley Review

I am also grateful to my friends, family, and teachers for educating and inspiring me, to Don Welch and Susan Aizenberg for their example, kindness, and generosity, David Rozema for encouraging my earliest work, Amy O'Reilly for reading an early draft of this manuscript, Chad Christensen for giving this book a perfect home, Dayla Lutz for asking for more poems during Icelandic storms, Katie Meuser for gifting the cover of this book, and most of all to my sons and my husband, for everything.

ABOUT THE AUTHOR

Kassandra Montag is an award-winning poet, novelist and essayist. Her work has appeared in journals and anthologies such as *Midwestern Gothic, Nebraska Poetry, Prairie Schooner,* and *Mystery Weekly Magazine.* Her debut novel, *After the Flood,* has been published in fourteen languages and has been optioned for television. She lives in Omaha, Nebraska with her husband and two sons.